How to drive a car

A handbook for responsible driving

Copyright

Table of content

INTRODUCTION

Congratulations! You're now ready to hit the broad road! However, before you can hit the road, you must first learn how to drive a vehicle. But don't worry; driving isn't tough; all it takes is a little knowledge and practice. We've included some basic guidelines below to assist you on your way - both literally and metaphorically!

The fundamental fundamentals of starting and shifting through the gears are simple enough for almost anybody to grasp. To drive a manual, you must get acquainted with the clutch, become acquainted with the gearstick, and practice starting, stopping, and changing gears at varied speeds.

Part 1

Learning the Fundamentals

Step 1.

Understand what each important component of a manual automobile does.

1. The shifter - The shifter is normally situated right above the transmission, in the middle of the car, between the driver and passenger seats. To change and pick the required gear in the gearbox, you will use your hand to control the shifter. The shifter will be used to choose Reverse, Neutral, 1st gear, 2nd gear, 3rd gear, and so on.

2. The clutch pedal - The clutch pedal is to the left of the brake pedal. To be used with the left foot. The clutch pedal activates the clutch mechanism, which links the engine to the gearbox. Whether the clutch pedal is in the up position (toward the driver), the gearbox is linked to the engine, and the car will be driven by the engine whether in forward or backward gear. If the clutch pedal is depressed (toward the floorboard), the engine and gearbox are disconnected, and the car does not get power from the engine.

3. The parking brake/handbrake - The parking brake is normally activated by hand and is positioned in the center console, however it may sometimes be located near the floor and actuated by foot.

The parking brake is NOT the same as the brake pedal. If the brake pedal is not depressed, the parking brake prevents the car from rolling while in neutral. While the ignition is turned off and the car is parked, the parking brake will be applied to keep it motionless.

Step 2.
Begin on level ground with the automobile turned off, gearbox in neutral, and parking brake applied.

Start carefully and deliberately, especially if this is your first time driving a vehicle with a manual gearbox. Once seated, fasten your seat belt. It might be beneficial to roll down the windows while studying. This allows you to hear the engine revving and swap gears appropriately.

The clutch is on the left, the brake is in the center, and the accelerator is on the right (remember it as C-B-A from left to right). This configuration applies to both left- and right-hand drive automobiles.

Step 3.

Discover what the clutch does.

Before you begin pressing this foreign pedal on the left, take a minute to learn the fundamentals of its operation.

- The clutch is what disconnects the engine from the wheels. When one or both spin, the clutch lets you to change gears without crushing the teeth of each individual gear.
- The clutch must be depressed (pushed) before changing gears (either up or down).

Step 4
Adjust your seat so that you have full access to the clutch pedal's range of motion.

Slide forward far enough to enable you to completely depress the clutch pedal (the left pedal next to the brake pedal) with your left foot.

Step 5. **Press and hold the clutch pedal to the floor.**
This is also an excellent moment to notice how the clutch pedal travel varies from the brake and gas pedals. It's also an excellent time to practice gently and gradually releasing the clutch pedal.

If you've only driven automatic automobiles, using your left foot to press a pedal may seem strange. With practice, you'll get used to utilizing both feet simultaneously.

Step 6.
Select neutral with the gearstick.

This is the neutral posture that allows you to move freely from side to side. When the car is regarded to be out of gear.

- The gearstick is set to neutral, and/or
- The clutch pedal has been depressed completely.
- It will not operate if you use the gearstick without first depressing the clutch pedal.

Step 7.
Start the engine with the key in the ignition while keeping the gear stick in neutral. Before starting the automobile, make sure the handbrake is engaged, particularly if you are a beginner.

- Some automobiles will start in neutral without pressing the clutch, while some later models will not.

Step 8.
Take your foot off the clutch pedal while the vehicle is still in neutral.

If you're on flat ground, you should stay still; if you're on a slope, you'll start rolling. If you're ready to start driving, be sure you let go of the handbrake (if it's engaged) before you start.

Part 2

Moving Ahead, In First Gear

1. Press the clutch pedal to the floor and shift into first gear. It should be at the upper-left position, with a visual arrangement of the gear pattern on top of the gearstick.

Gear patterns differ, so spend some time ahead studying your vehicle's gear scheme. You should practice shifting through the gears with the engine turned off (but the clutch engaged).

2. Lift your foot slowly off the clutch pedal. Continue to press it in until you hear the engine speed begin to reduce. Repeat this multiple times until you can identify the sound quickly. This is the issue of contention.

When swapping gears to get started or remain going, you'll want to have the accelerator down sufficiently to produce power.

3. Release the clutch while pressing the accelerator. Lift your left foot off the clutch pedal until the RPMs begin to decrease significantly. Apply mild pressure on the accelerator with your right foot at the same time. Balance the mild downward pressure on the accelerator with the gentle release of clutch pedal pressure. You'll probably have to do this numerous times before you get the correct balance of up and down pressure.

Another method is to release the clutch until the engine revs down little, then apply pressure to the accelerator as the clutch engages. The automobile will begin to move at this moment. The engine should be revved just enough to avoid stalling when the clutch pedal is released. Because you are unfamiliar with the additional pedal in a manual automobile, this procedure may be challenging at first.

Once you start driving forward under control in first gear, completely release the clutch (that is, carefully lift your foot from the pedal).

4. Expect to stall at least once when you initially start off. The engine will stall if you let off of the clutch too fast. If the engine sounds like it's about to stall, keep the clutch in place or press down a little more. If you stall, depress the clutch completely, apply the handbrake, shift into neutral, turn off the engine, and restart the vehicle normally. Don't freak out.

Revving the engine when the clutch is between completely up and totally depressed may prematurely wear down the clutch components, resulting in slippage or smoke at the gearbox. This is known as clutch riding and should be avoided.

Part 3

Stopping and shifting in motion

1. Recognize when it is time to move up a gear. When your RPMs hit about 2500 to 3000 while driving, it's time to move to the next gear, such as second if you're presently in first. However, the exact RPMs at which shifting is necessary will vary depending on the vehicle. Your engine will start to race and accelerate, and you must learn to identify this sounds.

Depress the clutch pedal until it disengages, then direct the gearstick straight down from first gear into the bottom-left position (usually second gear).

Some automobiles include a "Shift Light" or tachometer indicators that notify you when you need to shift so you don't overrun the engine.

2. Gently press down on the accelerator while gently releasing the clutch pedal. Moving gears while in motion is the same as moving into first at a standstill. It's all about hearing, watching, and feeling for the engine's indications, as well as having the right up-and-down time of your feet on the pedals. You'll get the hang of it if you keep practicing.

Once in gear and on the accelerator, remove your foot entirely from the clutch pedal. Resting your foot on the clutch pedal is a poor habit since it puts pressure to the clutch mechanism, causing the clutch to wear out prematurely.

3. As you slow down, shift down into a lower gear. Though you drive too slowly for the gear you're in, your vehicle will tremble as though it's ready to stall. To change down gears while driving, repeat the procedure of depressing the clutch and releasing the accelerator, moving gears (say, from third to second), then releasing the clutch while depressing the accelerator.

4. Come to an abrupt halt. To come to a complete halt in first gear, gently shift down until you reach it. When you're ready to come to a full stop, shift your right foot from the accelerator to the brake pedal and push down as hard as you can. The automobile will begin to shake and vibrate as you slow to around 10 mph (16 km/h). To avoid stalling, depress the clutch pedal completely and shift the gearstick into neutral. To come to a full halt, use the brake pedal.

You may also come to a complete stop in any gear by completely compressing the clutch and using the brake while shifting into neutral. This should be done only when you need to stop fast, since it gives you less control of the car.

Part 4

Troubleshooting and Practice

1. Run a simple course with an experienced manual driver. While you may legally practice alone on any public road with a valid driver's license, you will learn the complexities of driving a manual automobile quicker if you are accompanied by an experienced driver. Begin in a level, secluded place, such as a huge (and empty) parking lot, then go to calm suburban streets. Drive around the same circuit many times until you remember the varied abilities required.

2. Avoid beginning and stopping on steep climbs at first. Plan routes that avoid traffic signals at the tops of steep hills if you're new to driving a manual. To prevent drifting backwards while shifting into first gear, your timing and synchronization with the gear stick, clutch, brake, and accelerator must be reasonably quick.

You must be able to transfer your right foot rapidly (yet smoothly) from releasing the brake to applying the accelerator while also letting out the clutch. If necessary, apply the parking brake to minimize backward drifting, but remember to remove it as soon as you begin going ahead.

3. Understand parking procedures, particularly on slopes. Manual gearbox autos, unlike automatics, do not have a "park" gear. However, merely shifting into neutral allows your automobile to roll freely, particularly if parked on an incline or descent. Use the handbrake whenever possible, but don't depend on it to hold your vehicle in place when parked.

If you are parked facing uphill, turn off the engine and move into first gear before applying the parking brake. If you're going downhill, do the same thing but in reverse. This will prevent the wheels from rolling in the slope's direction.

To impede movement on steep inclines or merely to be extra careful, install chocks (angled blocks) behind your wheels.

4. Completely stop before switching from forward to reverse (and vice versa). Making a full stop while changing directions is a simple technique to avoid the possibility of inflicting costly damage to your gearbox.

It is highly advised to come to a full stop before shifting from reverse to first gear. However, most manual transmissions allow you to change into first or maybe second gear while driving backwards at a slow speed, although this is not advised since it might cause excessive clutch wear.

Some automobiles include a lock out system that prevents you from mistakenly activating reverse gear. Before operating the reverse gear, be sure you understand this locking mechanism and how to release it.

Tips

1. Learn to understand your engine's noises; you should ultimately be able to discern when to shift gears without using the rev meter.

2. If you're having trouble starting the automobile from a stop, check sure you're gently releasing the clutch. Stop at the friction point (when the engine begins to move the vehicle) and gently take the clutch out.

3. If your vehicle seems to be about to stall or the engine is sputtering, press the clutch again, wait for the engine to return to idle, and then repeat the starting procedure.

Caution

Until you're experienced driving a manual, keep an eye on the tachometer. A manual gearbox demands more knowledge than an automated transmission. Over revving the engine may cause significant engine damage.

Stop entirely before shifting into reverse, regardless of which way the automobile is moving. Shifting into reverse while driving will destroy most manual transmissions.

When you've stalled and restarted the engine many times, attempt to give the starter and battery a five to ten minute respite. This may assist to minimize overheating, starting damage, and entirely depleting the battery.

Keep an eye out if you're on a slope or in a hilly terrain. If you don't retain the brake and clutch, you might roll back and strike the person or item behind you.

How to Operate an Automatic Vehicle

After spending your whole driving career behind the wheel of a manual gearbox, an automatic transmission may appear perplexing. But, if you have the hang of it, automatics are far easier to operate than manuals. You've come to the perfect place if you're ready to drive an automatic for the first time and have questions about it! Continue reading to learn how to start an automatic, get it going, and park it once you get at your destination. And, if you've never driven a car before, have an experienced driver with you as you learn the basics.

What You Should Know

What You Should Understand

Use your right foot to hit the brake before you start the car.

Move the gearshift from P (park) to D (drive) to move ahead, or from R (reverse) to move backward.

Keep the car in drive at all times when you are driving. The automatic transmission selects the gear that matches the vehicle's speed the best.

Put the car in P (park) before turning the ignition off and applying the parking brake.

Part 1

Starting an Automatic Vehicle

Step 1
Adjust your seat and mirrors, then buckle up.

When you climb into the driver's seat, make sure your right foot can fully press the accelerator and brake pedals. If necessary, adjust your seat, then check your mirrors for visibility. Then buckle your seatbelt.

Examine the interior and become acquainted with the layout of the vehicle. This allows you to find the various indicator lights, headlights, windshield wipers, and other amenities when the vehicle is stationary.

If you can't locate what you're looking for, don't be afraid to look in the car's handbook (it's generally in the glove box, but if not, you can probably get a digital copy online).

Step 2
The brake pedal should be pressed with your right foot.

First and foremost, safety! Some automatic vehicles will start even if your foot is not on the brake pedal, but many will not. Every time, you want to do it. This allows you to double-check that the automobile isn't moving.

Step 3
To start the automobile, turn the key or press the button.

As you start the engine, keep your foot on the brake. Now when you're moving, take another look about you—turn on the headlights if necessary, connect your phone, adjust the climate controls, whatever you need to do to stay comfortable and stable on the road.

Step 4

To exit the parking place, put the car in D or R. Insert the lock button, which is normally located on the side or top of your shifter. Then, if you need to go forward, shift it from P (park) to D (drive), or R (reverse) if you need to back out. When you align the shifter with the proper gear, you'll hear a click. You can now proceed by releasing the button.

Take your hand off the gearshift completely—especially when driving.

If you're used to driving a manual, you probably rest your hand a lot on the shifter. You don't even need to swap gears when driving!

Step 5

Before you begin driving, let go of the parking brake.
Typically, the parking brake is a lever located adjacent to the gear change. To make the lever flush, press the button at the end of it. Make sure you don't let up on the brake! When the parking brake is depressed, the automobile will begin to roll as soon as you release it.

The parking brake is a pedal on the floor in various vehicles, particularly trucks and SUVs. Unless there's a separate brake release lever next to it, you'll normally push the pedal to release it.

Before you let off of the parking brake, put your automobile in drive. Because you're not depending on your transmission to keep your automobile in place, this eliminates unneeded wear and strain on it. This is especially critical if you are parked on a slope.

Part 2

Driving an Automatic Vehicle

Step 1
While driving, leave the car in D.

This is maybe the finest thing about driving an automatic! You don't have to bother with the gear shifter once you're on the road. Regardless matter your tempo, maintain it in D. Your car will automatically pick and move to the proper gear based on your speed.

An autonomous vehicle steers in the same way as a manual vehicle. In actuality, driving an automatic vehicle is comparable to driving a manual car—you just don't have to shift gears.

If this is your first time driving a vehicle, take it gently and turn the steering wheel in the direction you want the car to drive. You can do it!

Step 2

Press the accelerator and brake with your right foot. You're already aware with this method if you've driven a car with a manual transmission—you used your right foot for the accelerator and brake, and your left foot for the clutch. Drive an automatic in the same way, sans the clutch pedal. Most automatic automobiles contain a footrest (also called as a "dead pedal") on the left where you may rest your left foot.

True, Formula One drivers brake with their left foot. They are also highly skilled drivers who employ automobiles specifically adapted for this strategy. Simply stop and accelerate with your right foot while keeping your left foot to the side.

Be extra careful if you're driving a vehicle with a parking brake pedal on the floor.

It'll generally be off to the left side, so you won't mistake it for a clutch, but you should be aware of it.

Tuck your left foot beneath your right foot and out of the way if your left foot tends to wander toward the pedals while driving—problem solved!

Step3

If you need to reverse, put the car in reverse.

Make a complete stop and retain your foot on the brake. Then, on the shifter, click the button and move it close to the R. When you let off of the brake, you will be in reverse.

As soon as you let off of the brake, your car will begin to creep. When driving in reverse, you may take advantage of this—you won't need to do much more than lightly touch the pedal.

Remember that when you maneuver your car in reverse, the rear wheels will travel in the opposite direction that you turn the steering wheel. Turn left to return to the right, then right to return to the left.

Step 4

When you need less speed and more power, consider lower gears.

Your car's gearbox may have L below the D, or it may have a "1" and a "2" (for first and second gear). Shifting from D to L retains your car in a lower gear.

This is a function you'll only use occasionally, if at all, but it comes in helpful when you need it. Utilize the lowest gear level in the following situations:

Tugging: offers you a lot greater power for short distances if you're pulling something.

Winter weather conditions: enhances tire traction and prevents wheels from spinning out of control.

Extremely steep hills: less effort on your engine going uphill, less wear and tear on your brakes heading downhill.

Step 5

Avoid N unless your car is being towed. In a manual vehicle, you're in neutral a lot—basically, anytime you stop.

However, not in an automated! Automatic automobiles contain a neutral gear ("N" on your gearbox), but you'll rarely use it.

Some people assume that moving your car into neutral when stopped at traffic signals will aid you preserve gas. However, any fuel savings are, at best, modest. All you're doing is putting additional (and needless) wear and tear to your transmission.

Part 3

How to Park an Automatic Vehicle

Step 1:

Put the car in reverse to park into a parking area.

It's normally safer to reverse into a parking area, unless there's a local rule or a parking lot restriction. In an automatic transmission car, merely come to a complete stop with your foot on the brake and shift into R. Remove your foot off the brake and put it on the accelerator, then lightly push the pedal to slowly return to the required space.

Step 2

You must pull the lever to engage the parking brake.

Keep your foot on the brake to prevent your car from rolling. Pull the lever up until you hear it click, then press the button at the end of it. If you pull it up too far, it may become stuck—you'll know when it's engaged. Take your hand off the lever and let go of the button.

If your parking brake has a pedal on the floor, depress it fully to engage the parking brake.

When you're not sure whether you've applied the parking brake, carefully raise your foot off the brake. It is not triggered if the car starts to roll.

It's ideal for your gearbox if you utilize the parking brake before shifting gears.

Step 3
Release the brake and put the car in park.

Push the lock button on the shifter's side all the way to the P position. The vehicle stays in this gear while parked; unlike a manual car, it is not put in neutral. Just remember that P stands for "park" to avoid making that blunder.

Step 4

If you're parked on a hill, spin the wheel.

If you're parked on a steep slope, this gives some extra safety in case your brakes fail or someone touches your car and it starts to move. In general, if you're parking downhill, turn your wheels toward the curb, and if you're parked uphill, spin your wheels away from the curb.

Turn your wheels if you've parked into a sloping driveway so your car doesn't slip out onto the road.

Step5

Turn off the car. You're done! Turn the key or push the button to leave the car and congratulate yourself on your first successful drive in an automatic transmission vehicle. Take the keys with you and remember to lock the doors.

CONCLUSION

Driving is a voyage of responsibility, awareness, and profound comprehension of the road. It involves more than merely controlling pedals and steering the wheels.

"How to drive a car" is more than just a user manual; it's also a manual for developing a competent, thoughtful way to move through life's ever-evolving terrain. Keep in mind that each turn is a metaphor for the detours life may take you on as the motor hums and the tire rolls. So fasten your seatbelts, keep alert, and enjoy the journey.

Printed in Great Britain
by Amazon

34891393R00020